Becoming Debt Free!

by Anthony Rossetti

Copyright © 2017 Anthony Rossetti

All rights reserved. No part of this publication may be reproduced, distributed, or transmitted in any form or by any means, including photocopying, recording, or other electronic or mechanical methods, without the prior written permission of the publisher, except in the case of brief quotations embodied in critical reviews and certain other noncommercial uses permitted by copyright law.

Table of Contents

Introduction

I. Rude Awakening

II. Overspending

III. Forget the "Jones Family"

IV. The Credit Card Trap

V. Entering the Adult Workforce

VI. 30 Year Mortgage vs. 15 Year

VII. Home Equity

VIII. Budgeting

IX. Determination, Commitment, Self-Control

X. Reaping the Reward

Introduction

Becoming Debt Free is about my life's journey to free myself from the burden of debt. I want to share this information with you because it's not really about me but about how the methodology I have accepted and put into practice can help you to do the same. Our financial habits are developed at a young age and play a critical role throughout our lifetime. It was not until more recent years that schools began requiring students to take a class on life and financial skills. Many people are never given any formal type of education about managing finances and the various intricacies involved in balancing life and debt.

I have great news for those who dream of the freedom of not having to pay banks and credit card companies your entire life. I've discovered a way to do it and have become debt free. I am not wealthy and have not had any formal training. I'm just an average guy who has worked hard and devoted myself to a series of goals. That being said, I could not have achieved this goal without the hard work and support of my wife.

My wife has played a critical role in reaching our goal of being debt free. We met in college with the like-minded goal of obtaining our degrees and finding careers to support ourselves in our adult lives. I believe it is important to be around like-minded people who share your values and encourage you. This is especially true when dating and becoming serious with someone who you have the potential of sharing your life with. My wife and I have a child who is the joy of our life and is truly a blessing. It's necessary I mention our family of three because raising a child is very costly. We have been through 7 years of daycare, nursery school, childcare and summer camp expenses that have been a large part of our monthly budget.

The purpose of this book is to share with you and hopefully generate thought as to how you can use my knowledge and experience in order to better your financial life. I am a true believer that if one individual can do it, so can another. I've learned that most great things do not come easy and require hard work, but you get out what you put in and the lifetime reward of being debt free is a worthy and realistic goal.

I. Rude Awakening

As far back as I can remember, my basic financial skills were taught to me by my parents. I can recall saving money in my piggy bank like most kids. When I was given money for a birthday, holiday or my grandpa would visit and give me a dollar it went straight into my piggy bank. Of course it's easy to save when you're a child because you're unemployed and cared for by adults.

There is usually one spouse in the relationship who manages the finances and most often it's because that spouse is better at it. Money can be a challenge in a relationship and is a common cause for marital problems. It is important to figure out early in the relationship which spouse is better suited for managing the finances. In my house that was my mother. I vaguely but specifically remember my mother taking me to open my first bank account. It was a savings account and I liked the idea of continuously depositing money in it and watching it grow.

Eventually, as I got older and began working, I recall opening my first checking account in addition to my savings account. I remember my mom sitting down with me and showing me how to balance a check book. Now that I was earning some money I had to learn how to budget it. Here is the simple rule I learned that very day. You must always deposit more money than you withdraw. Sounds simple, but don't you know someone who occasionally overdrafts their checking account? I have known a number of people who have and I am happy to say I have never overdrawn my checking account. If you balance your check book and manage your finances you should know you're close to withdrawing too much from your checking account and at least transfer money from your savings account.

My mother taught me that as soon as I deposit my paycheck I should come up with a set amount I am comfortable with and immediately transfer it to my savings account. I didn't know it then, but it is a rule I've read in many financial articles in my adult life called "pay your-self first". This rule is not about grabbing a handful of cash and going out to spoil yourself silly because you worked hard for it. It's about setting aside money for your savings before you pay your bills and other expenses. If the money is left in your checking account it's easy to view it as spending cash and often times will be spent. A savings account is a very simple way to set aside money from your spendable cash. I've read various studies that claim nearly 50% of Americans are living paycheck to paycheck. I have a hard time accepting this because I grew up with the mentality to save for a rainy day. Unfortunately, there is the realization that some people make very little money and struggle to save let alone make ends-meat. People lose jobs, get divorced and financial turmoil does occur. However, most of the time when you are working you should be able to set aside at least a small amount of savings.

Although I credit my mom for my basic budgeting skills, my dad has always been a major role model for me. My father has always had a strong work ethic which he instilled in me. My mom stayed home with my brother and me when we were younger so we spent more time with her. My father worked all day and even worked part time at night at certain times in my childhood. He wanted to make sure his family was financially taken care of and he has always been a great provider. Nothing makes a stronger impression than leading by example. Eventually, my mom went back to work full time as my brother and I got older and both my parents still work fulltime today. I'm giving you some of my background so that you can understand the type of work ethic and support I've had which has lead me to my debt free life. I understand not everyone has this type of upbringing which makes it harder to learn in adulthood, but it can be done and I'm going to explain how.

Saving money is only a means to affording something greater. There is no point in hoarding money with no goal in sight. Goal setting is critical in order to establish a sense of focus. I set my first major financial goal in my teenage years when I committed myself to buying my first car. I had been saving for about ten years and I was finally going to use my money for something great. I remember seeing a used car with a "for sale" sign and my dad and I contacted the seller. We then went to see the car and test drive it. My dad negotiated a sale price pending we get it inspected by a mechanic. The mechanic told us it was in pretty good shape for a 12 year old car with 102,000 miles and only needed a couple of minor repairs. Success! My goal of paying for my first car was a tremendous achievement and I was proud of myself.

At this point in my life, everything I had purchased was something I paid for once and owned. Shortly after I purchased the car I brought it back to the same mechanic who had given me a price quote for the repairs it needed. I was told the repairs should be made in a couple of days and they'd call me when it was ready. When I went to pick it up the mechanic had made an additional repair which I was not informed of and my repair totaled somewhere around $500. I was shocked that after spending the large majority of my savings on the car, I now had to pull more money out of savings for an even bigger repair then I expected. Thankfully I had enough to cover the repair but there wasn't much leftover. I explained to my dad that I didn't expect it to cost so much and I was frustrated to have to use more of the money I had saved so diligently. My dad listened until I was done venting and said, "That's just how cars are". This was my rude awakening. I had reached a point in my life where I realized big purchases often come with re-curing expenses. As an adult there are many re-curing expenses which play a critical role in budgeting, but I'll discuss this in greater detail later. This story was a pivotal moment in my financial mindset and has impacted me to this day. Nonetheless, I was proud of my achievement and I still remember the pride I felt as I washed that car every week in my parent's driveway.

II. Overspending

    Spending habits are learned behaviors we develop early in our lives. Most of our early experiences with spending money were taught to us by our parents or guardians. I've observed a number of different people with variations of learned and developed spending behaviors. The more straightforward are people who have similar spending and financial habits to that of their parents. I know people that have financial struggles on a regular basis and have gone into some depth about how they manage money. You don't often get into budgeting discussions with people unless you're fairly close. I can tell immediately where they are mismanaging their money. As it turns out, their parents have had the same lifetime of struggle. Unfortunately, their parents' poor habits have impacted them negatively in their financial life. I have given useful advice to some that have used it with great success. However, there are others that are too stuck in their ways and continue to spend frivolously.

    I have also run into the exact opposite types of people that have learned positive spending habits from their parents. Lucky for them to have had a good education on spending, but not everyone does. The more interesting types of people are those that have developed spending habits in opposition to the way they were raised. It's not uncommon for people who have grown up in a small house or apartment with parents that were cautious with money to want the greater things in life once they reach adulthood. There's absolutely nothing wrong with wanting a better future for your family either. Where it becomes a problem is when people overspend and over consume. Have you ever gotten rid of something that you thought, "What a waste of money? Why did I buy that in the first place?" I certainly have and it wasn't until I was getting rid of it that I realized it was a poor decision to spend my hard earned money on it.

    I usually research what I'm thinking of buying in order to make the most informed decision. Buyer's remorse is not a good feeling especially when you purchase something you can't return. Often times I will consider how many hours I had to work in order to purchase the item I'm considering. It can help put into perspective the amount of time you sacrificed in order to make a purchase. Another useful tip is to ask yourself if you really need the item you're thinking of purchasing and do you think it will continue to be of use in the future. If not, maybe it isn't worth buying. Besides, who needs all the extra clutter in their home? I like things to look neat and inviting when I walk into my house. I don't want to walk into a room cluttered with useless objects. Some people have a true addiction to spending money because they like how it makes them feel when they buy something new. Unfortunately, the feeling wears off pretty quickly and one might find themselves feeling unfulfilled. Keeping up that high can be very expensive. I personally enjoy saving money by foregoing the less important things in order to be able to afford something more important in the future.

I think most of us can agree that we don't exactly desire to live life like a monk and shed all earthly possessions. However, there is something to be said for minimizing the burden and attachment to material things. I can recall selling an item and feeling a sense of relief once it was gone. Apparently, the item I sold had possessed me more than I ever possessed it. I don't think that is a very healthy way to feel about material things. Maybe sometimes we put too much emotional attachment into objects and should try harder to focus our emotions on something more life fulfilling.

III. Forget the "Jones Family"

As human beings we tend to be competitive. When we're children we compete for our parents' attention. Children like to be in the limelight and often times become jealous when another child steals the show. As children grow up they are constantly in competition in the never ending race to outcompete their peers. Whether it's school or sports the goal is to improve and outperform others. This sense of competition is a part of life and continues well into our adult careers. It can be especially apparent when it comes to money. There are many people who feel they have to show their financial success by flaunting it which often comes in the form of large or flashy purchases or even outright bragging. If we're always trying to top others where does it end? Do you have to have a bigger house, nicer car or fancier clothes? These are personal preferences but you have to have the extra money to be able to purchase this lifestyle.

      I grew up in a middle class town in Northern New Jersey. Many people in town worked in Manhattan and made a lot of money. I was very used to seeing expensive cars and houses in town. In high school it became apparent that many people liked to exude a sense of financial success. A number of my peers were given new cars when they turned 17 and some were very expensive. What's tricky about the appearance of having money is that you don't need to have a lot of it to be able to finance or lease an expensive looking vehicle. I realized the parents' of my peers were financing or leasing these fancy cars in order to show their family had money. I'm sure some of them did but in my adult years I've come to know many people who lease expensive cars and really don't have the money they're trying to perpetrate. I didn't care about the fancy cars in the parking lot that were given to some of my peers with no actual effort on their part. I was proud of my 12 year old car that I earned. Which brings me to the main point of this chapter; don't worry about keeping up with the Joneses. If it is important to you to have a nicer car than your neighbor then by all means go for it. However, if you don't have much extra money to put away in savings and decide to finance the fancy car you are overspending. Usually this type of overspending is not an isolated incident but a repetitive behavior. Let's say you finance a house and a few years later your income has grown. Then you decide to sell your house and take on a bigger mortgage for a larger house. You may have increased your income which is always a good thing, but you've also increased your debt. This pattern of overspending prevents people from being able to save and invest.

Often times increasing debt in order to outcompete others will continue to grow and even outpace your income growth. If you or your spouse loses a job it can put you in a disastrous situation. Having money in savings is very important for this very type of situation. It has been suggested in a number of articles I've read to have at least six months of living expenses in savings. This allows you up to six months to find a job before you have to liquidate your assets. This is often referred to as an 'Emergency Fund'. If you are in the habit of overspending it can be very difficult to save six months of living expenses.

Besides the financial burden of trying to keep up with your friends or neighbors, there's also a feeling of emptiness that comes with always wanting more things. It's hard to find contentment in life when you're constantly thinking about the next expensive purchase. I live in a moderate sized house. It's got the space my family needs and is not excessive. I own it outright with no mortgage and could certainly sell it and buy a bigger house. My wife and I worked hard to pay off our mortgage and don't want to take out another one. We like our home and are content and grateful for what we have. I absolutely feel a sense of peace in being happy with what I have instead of the empty feeling of wanting more. I don't expect you to want to adopt my exact way of doing things but I think it's important for all of us to find our own balance that makes us happy.

IV. The Credit Card Trap

     The first piece of credit most of us obtain is a credit card. Usually that is because you are approved for a smallcredit limit and credit card companies can afford to take the risk of a small dollar amount on someone that has no credit history. However, young people should be especially careful when it comes to credit card companies. Credit card companies seem like they line up to send you offers as soon as you reach 18 years old. I know 18 marks the legal age of adulthood, but many 18 year olds are not very financially responsible. Credit cards can be a real trap especially for young people. It's so easy to swipe a card, run up a substantial balance and then realize it's too much to pay back at the end of the month. In this type of situation you'd probably pay the minimum amount required and carry a balance into the next month.

     Where people get trapped is when they continue to use the credit card and the balance grows. Interest rates on credit cards are very high compared to most other types of loans. If you just make minimum payments you're mostly paying interest so the principal balance will be reduced very slowly. If you miss a payment the credit card company will charge a fee and could increase your interest rate. If you're late 60 days you could incur a penalty rate which can be close to 30%. This compounds the problem of not being able to pay down principal.

For example, let's say you have run up a $2,500 credit card balance. The national average interest rate on credit cards right now is approximately 15%, so we'll use that interest rate. The minimum payment is $25. If you make only the minimum monthly payment suggested by your credit card statement, by the time you pay off your $2,500 balance you will have made 172 payments (that's 14.33 years) and you will have paid $2,807.22 in interest charges! The interest payments alone will be more than the original balance. Now let us compare this using the same balance and interest rate but making the monthly payment of $50. With a monthly payment of $50 you will have made 79 payments (that's 6.58 years) and you will have paid $1,447.80 in interest charges. This is assuming you have discontinued using the credit card and have made all monthly payments on time avoiding a penalty rate or added fees. As you can see it's very difficult to pay off the original balance when making only the minimum suggested payment. When that payment was increased from $25 to $50 it reduced the term from 14.33 years to 6.58 years and saved $1,359.42 in interest. When it comes to loan payments I highly recommend paying a significant amount of additional principal.

The only thing worse than making minimum payments, is missing a payment altogether. Aside from a penalty rate and late fees, missed payments on any loan can cause damage to your credit report. It's important to have a good credit report not only for obtaining loans but also for getting the lowest possible interest rates. Lenders often use your credit score in determining what type of interest rate they can offer. The higher the score, the less interest you have to pay the bank and that's more money you can add to your savings account.

Going back to my previous comment about credit card companies mailing credit card offers to young adults. Credit card companies love to solicit college students. I've seen them on college campuses offering free giveaways to fill out and submit a credit application. I remember visiting a friend in their college dorm room and seeing a credit card lying in a pile of clutter which still had an activation sticker on it. I asked why they had the card lying around. My friend told me they had the card for a couple of years but never activated it. So I asked why they would apply for a credit card if they didn't need it. My friend said they filled out the application because they were offered a free t-shirt. Luckily that friend is very responsible but I've met others that have run up credit cards and have been caught in the trap.

My advice on credit cards is not to use them. I keep a credit card for emergencies and only use it occasionally for certain travel, insurance and product warranty benefits the credit card company offers. I rarely use it because it's really not your money you're paying with. We don't always think of it as a loan because once we have the credit card it's so readily available and easy to use, but a loan is exactly what it is. Some people like taking advantage of credit card reward programs but you have to be extremely disciplined and make sure you don't overspend and will pay the full balance every month.

I have a few suggestions if you've already been caught in the credit card trap. First, stop using the credit card. You know yourself better than anyone else. If you can't control yourself than you may want to take the card(s) out of your wallet and hide them somewhere you won't touch them. If you know that won't work, cut them up. Your accounts will not be closed and credit lines still intact, but you won't be able to run up the balance. Make sure you cancel any automatic charges to the card(s) and remove them as a payment option from any internet sites where you shop. Next, assess how much you owe and how much of your payment(s) go to interest. Then, determine how much additional principal you can afford to pay on a monthly basis. Figure out the math and determine how long it will take you to pay off your credit card debt. Don't be ashamed to ask someone for help. You're looking to improve your life and that's nothing to be ashamed of. Lastly, stay committed. You have to make that payment every month for as long as it takes. Even if it's hard to see the end in sight; stay committed. Math doesn't lie and if you calculated the payment correctly you will get yourself out of credit card debt.

V. Entering the Adult Workforce

Most of us have probably had jobs in high school and college, but those wages are usually not livable wages. Whether you've just graduated college or completed high school you now are entering the adult workforce. A lot of romanticized truths start to become apparent when you start working a full time job. Expectations you may have had are put in check and reality kicks in. Your first couple paychecks are the largest you've ever received and you're proud and excited. Naturally you have this new money you've never had before and you have to decide what to do with it. I've seen a number of young people go out and finance a new car. Hopefully, they bought something moderately within their means because they have now added to their debt. I don't recommend taking on an unnecessary debt unless you absolutely have to in order to get to work. What I do suggest is to buy a used car that you can either pay for with savings or only take out a small, short-term loan. One of the biggest problems with auto loans is that you can be persuaded to take a longer term loan in order to make the payment smaller. However, vehicles depreciate (lose value) quickly meaning you could end up owing more money on the car than it's worth. This can prevent you from being able to sell or trade it in the future.

I've known others who have focused their early paychecks on paying down student loan debt. If you can come up with a budget that allows you to pay your student loan debt off earlier in life, it will free up cash for your future. Student loan minimums are similar to credit card minimums. Student loans can be amortized (reduce by making payments) to pay off anywhere from 10 to 30 years. The more aware you are about money early in life the better off you'll be. Fortunately, I was a saver in my young life and never ran up credit card debt. After about six months out of college, while working, I decided to buy a condo. This was my first debt which I will discuss a bit later. My wife, then girlfriend, was completing her Master's Degree and I proposed to her a few months later. She and I had discussed money and finance while dating and decided to not use credit cards so we had no credit card debt. We decided to devote both of our paychecks to paying down student loan debt and saving what we could for a wedding after paying a mortgage and living expenses.

At the time my wife was commuting to work which became difficult, so we found a used car for about $10,000 and put down a $1,000. We now had a mortgage, student loans and a small car loan. In about one to two years' time I had gone from having no financial obligations to having somewhere around $200,000 in debt. This is a big number but much has to be taken into account. There is a difference between good debt and bad debt. Credit cards are bad debts. They are not a necessity and are mostly harmful if you can't afford to pay them off. Student loans are an example of good debt because they afford you the opportunity to get the education needed in order to obtain a career with a good salary. It's important to be aware of student loan debt because it's often overlooked when you're beginning college and don't have to worry about making payments for another four years. You can make the conscious decision to attend a college that is less costly. In my case, I commuted to a local state university which is much less expensive than living on campus. My wife went to the same university and was fortunate enough to have a scholarship. The student loan debt came later when she pursued and completed her Master's Degree. She made the decision to finance the higher degree because it was a worthwhile investment. A mortgage is another good debt because we all need somewhere to live and it is an asset you own and build equity in. The money is not spent and gone as with a credit card. A mortgage is a large, usually the largest, expense you have and carries with it a lot of additional expenses such as maintenance, property tax, insurance and mortgage interest. However, a portion of your mortgage payment always goes to principal and that builds you equity in your home. In essence your home is like a savings account in that you make contributions over time and can accumulate a large amount of cash when it's sold.

VI. 30 Year Mortgage vs. 15 Year

Many of us share the dream of homeownership, but how knowledgeable are we when buying our first home? We get advice from our parents or someone we know with more life experience. Has anyone ever sat down with you and explained the different financing options prior to beginning the process of purchasing a home? I was fortunate enough to receive some guidance prior to purchasing my first home which was a condo. I had a good understanding of how mortgages work and decided to take out a 30 year bi-weekly mortgage. The reason I chose a bi-weekly mortgage is that you make payments every two weeks. A bi-weekly mortgage has a few different benefits. First, your payment is broken down almost in half so you make two smaller payments per month. Next, you pay down principal faster. By making payments every two weeks the interest paid is being reduced faster because you are paying principal down more frequently. Also, there are 26 bi-weekly payments in a 12 month period so you are actually making 13 payments per year. This also reduces principal quicker than if you were making 12 monthly payments.

You usually pay the most interest at the beginning of the loan because that is when the principal balance is the highest. Each payment you make reduces the principal amount. The next month the interest portion of your payment will decrease because it is calculated on the current month's principal balance. Since the payment is setup as a fixed payment by the mortgage company, the principal portion of your payment increases as the interest portion decreases. For example, let's say you take out a $100,000 mortgage with a 4% interest rate. We are not including any property taxes or insurance in order to keep this simple and focus on the principal and interest relationship. Table 1 displays an amortization schedule for the first year (12 months) of a 30 year mortgage. Notice how the principal portion of the payment increases each month as the interest portion decreases. The principal and interest relationship is important to be aware of in order to understand how additional principal payments can drastically reduce the amount of interest you pay.

Table 1: 30 year mortgage

Nbr	Payment	Principal	Interest	Ending Principal Balance
				$100,000.00
1	$477.42	$144.09	$333.33	$99,855.91
2	$477.42	$144.57	$332.85	$99,711.34
3	$477.42	$145.05	$332.37	$99,566.29
4	$477.42	$145.53	$331.89	$99,420.76
5	$477.42	$146.02	$331.40	$99,274.74
6	$477.42	$146.50	$330.92	$99,128.24
7	$477.42	$146.99	$330.43	$98,981.25
8	$477.42	$147.48	$329.94	$98,833.77
9	$477.42	$147.97	$329.45	$98,685.80
10	$477.42	$148.47	$328.95	$98,537.33
11	$477.42	$148.96	$328.46	$98,388.37
12	$477.42	$149.46	$327.96	$98,238.91

For comparison, let's look at table 2 which shows a 30 year bi-weekly mortgage compared to regular monthly payments. As you can see year-over-year the bi-weekly payment is higher because you are making one extra payment per year which in turn is reducing the principal balance faster. Notice the difference in the principal balance at the end of each year. At the end of year 1 the principal balance is $488 less than when making bi-weekly instead of monthly payments. At the end of year 2, the difference in the principal balance is $997. By the end of year 3, the difference in the principal balance is $1,526. As the loan progresses you can see how the compounding effect of bi-weekly payments reduces principal. This compounding effect continues to grow over the term of the loan.

Table 2: 30 year bi-weekly vs. monthly payments

Year	Bi-weekly Payments		Monthly Payments	
	Payments	Balance	Payments	Balance
		$100,000		$100,000
1	$6,206	$97,751	$5,729	$98,239
2	$6,206	$95,409	$5,729	$96,406
3	$6,206	$92,973	$5,729	$94,499

Table 3 shows how using accelerated bi-weekly payments reduces your total interest payments from $71,868 to $60,592 over the life of the loan. This is a total interest savings of $11,276. Not to mention this is assuming only a $100,000 mortgage. On a larger mortgage balance the interest savings is even greater. Also, some banks offer a slightly lower interest rate on a bi-weekly mortgage which reduces interest even further. Another great feature of the bi-weekly payment structure is that the term of the loan is reduced and pays off in 25.9 years instead of 30 years. There is little sacrifice on your part except you have to budget smaller payments every two weeks. The payments can be setup on automatic draft from your checking account. I highly recommend a bi-weekly mortgage because as you can see in our example you can save a lot of money and shorten the term of the mortgage by a few years.

Table 3:

	Bi-weekly Payments	**Monthly Payments**
Mortgage amount	$100,000	$100,000
Interest rate	4.000%	4.000%
Payment	$238.71 accelerated bi-weekly	$477.42 monthly
Years to repay	25.9 years	30 years
Total interest	$60,592	$71,868
Interest savings	$11,276	

Now that we understand the benefits of paying down principal faster, let's turn our attention to the 15 year mortgage. The 15 year mortgage is a huge interest saver, as long as you are comfortable making the higher monthly (or bi-weekly) payment. In Table 4 you'll see we have a comparison of a 15 year mortgage vs. 30 year mortgage. I am using the same $100,000 loan amount but am using a 3.25% interest rate for the 15 year mortgage and a 4% interest rate for the 30 year mortgage. I did not change the rate in my prior examples because we were comparing two different types of 30 years mortgages and the rate difference may be very little if any. The rate difference from a 30 to a 15 year term is very significant and in this case is a 0.75% difference which is realistic. As you can see a 15 year mortgage term will save you $45,388 in interest, but only if you can afford an additional $225 per month. That savings is a whopping 45% of your original loan amount.

Table 4: 15 year mortgage vs. 30 year mortgage

Mortgage Comparison		
	15 year mortgage	**30 year mortgage**
Loan amount	$100,000	$100,000
Interest rate	3.250%	4.000%
Monthly payment	$702.67	$477.42
Total interest	$26,480	$71,868
Total payments	$126,480	$171,868

Below are the payment schedules for the 15 year and 30 year payment schedules by year. Take a moment to study the differences. Notice how the interest as well as the principal reduces much quicker on the 15 year payment schedule. It's often advised to purchase a home only if you expect to live in it for a minimum of five years. If you take out a 15 year mortgage and decide to sell it after five years your principal balance will have been paid down to $71,906.94 as compared to $90,447.20 on a 30 year mortgage. That's a difference of $18,540.26.

15 Year Payment schedule

Year	Total Payments	Principal Paid	Interest Paid	Ending Principal Balance
				$100,000.00
1	$8,432.04	$5,259.94	$3,172.10	$94,740.06
2	$8,432.04	$5,433.44	$2,998.60	$89,306.62
3	$8,432.04	$5,612.70	$2,819.34	$83,693.92
4	$8,432.04	$5,797.86	$2,634.18	$77,896.06
5	$8,432.04	$5,989.12	$2,442.92	$71,906.94

30 Year Payment schedule

Year	Total Payments	Principal Paid	Interest Paid	Ending Principal Balance
				$100,000.00
1	$5,729.04	$1,761.09	$3,967.95	$98,238.91
2	$5,729.04	$1,832.85	$3,896.19	$96,406.06
3	$5,729.04	$1,907.53	$3,821.51	$94,498.53
4	$5,729.04	$1,985.22	$3,743.82	$92,513.31
5	$5,729.04	$2,066.11	$3,662.93	$90,447.20

With any budget goal there is a certain amount of sacrifice that must be made. I believe it's more beneficial to budget for a 15 year mortgage. I would even advise to buy a slightly less expensive house in order to afford the 15 year mortgage. 30 year mortgages essentially provide banks with a longer income stream which is only beneficial to the bank not the customer. There are also 15 year bi-weekly mortgages which have the same compound interest savings as our example in Table 2. 10 year terms exist but increase the payment even more. What I'd like you to take away from this chapter is that the shorter the term and more often you pay down principal, the more interest you save.

VII. Home Equity

Building equity in your home is the main reason people choose to own a home instead of renting. Every mortgage payment you make contributes to reducing the principal balance which increases the amount of equity you have in your home. You can use the equity in your home as collateral to obtain a home equity loan. Sometimes people take out home equity loans or lines in order to make home improvements, consolidate debt, purchase a vehicle or other various reasons. A home equity loan is a lump sum that is financed at a fixed rate for a fixed term. The terms usually range from 5 years up to 20 years. A home equity line of credit works similar to a credit card except you are given checks instead of a card. You can use the checks and the balance is drawn down against the line. There is a maximum credit line which you cannot exceed. The biggest negative of a home equity line is there is a variable rate which can increase over time. If you are thinking about taking out a home equity line be aware of what type of interest rate environment you are currently in. If you are in a rising interest rate environment it would probably be in your best interest to take out home equity loan since it is at a fixed rate.

Home equity loans/lines have advantages and disadvantages. They usually offer a lower interest rate because they are collateralized by your house. The interest is usually tax deductible which means you can use the interest expense to offset your taxable income when filing your taxes. This type of loan must be used wisely. If you have accumulated high interest debt (ex. credit cards) it is not a bad idea to consolidate and pay it off with a home equity. This will offer a lower interest rate so you can work on paying it off quicker and it offers a tax benefit. I know people that have used a home equity to purchase a vehicle instead of taking out an auto loan since the interest is tax deductible. I've used a home equity line of credit in order to refinance and payoff my mortgage. I chose to do so because there are little to no closing costs when taking out a home equity loan or line. Mortgages often have high closings costs which can make a home equity a better option for refinancing. I also had a very short term plan for when I would pay off the home equity line since it has a variable interest rate.

    What I don't like about home equity loans or lines is that it is technically a second mortgage. Taking out another loan goes against the goal of becoming debt free. Why pay down a mortgage and build equity only to take the equity back out of your house? This is why I said home equity loans/lines can be useful but only for the short term. My wife and I like to occasionally watch reality shows where they renovate homesand make home improvements. Oftentimes in these shows the renovation costs exceed the homeowner's budget and somehow they almost always manage to come up with the additional money. My wife and I are left wondering where they are getting the money from. We have to assume a good portion of the homeowners are taking out some type of home equity loan.

Here's where I've seen home equity loans come back to bite homeowners. Years ago before the "Great Recession", home values had skyrocketed. Homeowners saw their property values increase for a long period of time and they built a lot of equity simply from market appreciation. I remember seeing a lot of homes undergoing major renovations and remodels. When the "Great Recession" hit home values plummeted. Tens of thousands of homeowners found themselves in situations where they owed more money on their homes then they were worth (underwater). Those homeowners that had taken out second and third mortgages (home equity loans) were heavily underwater. During the recession many people lost their jobs. Many unemployed homeowners were unable to sell their homes since they were underwater. Jobs were scarceand people were unable to make their mortgage payments or sell their home so the banks were forced to foreclose on the properties. There were a record number of foreclosures during the "Great Recession". I learned a very important lesson about the importance of not taking equity out of your home. I don't recommend borrowing if it's not absolutely necessary. The more you borrow the further away you'll be from becoming debt free.

VIII. Budgeting

The education system's main goal is to prepare us for adult life. I can't understand why something as life impacting as learning to budget money has not been incorporated into our education system for hundreds of years. I can't speak for all schools but none of the grade schools I attended had any type of personal finance course. I remember learning to sew and cook but never how to manage money. I am happy to say that I have become aware in more recent years that there are high schools offering classes to teach students about money.

Budgeting is the process of allotting money for different purposes. You can setup numerous accounts and move money to them but I find it easier to have fewer accounts and keep track of my spending. Of course increasing your income as much as possible is helpful because you have to have income before you can setup a budget. Income and expenses are the two main components in any budget. My suggestion is to maximize your income and minimize your expenses. The greater the difference, the larger the cash flow. Cash flowis the money left over after all expenses are paid. This is where living within your means is very important.

The first step in creating a budget is to make a list starting with your income. Beneath your income include all of your expenses which are necessities. This includes food, clothes, utilities, housing expenses, car, insurances, cell phone and anything else that you absolutely need to pay. Now subtract your expenses from your income. The number leftover represents your discretionary income. If you have little or no money left over you are living above your means. Living above your means is a recipe for financial hardship but this is something that can be changed. You can make adjustments to your income and expenses in order to widen that gap. It's often easier to cut expenses than to increase income. I've cut my expenses by switching to a less expensive cell phone provider. I've also decreased my monthly utilities by cutting out cable and using less expensive streaming services. I installed programmable thermostats which have drastically reduced my gas and electric bills. In more extreme situations it may be necessary to downsize to a less expensive house, apartment or car. These are just some possible examples but the main idea is to make adjustments to your income and/or expenses in order to create more cash flow.

Another option is to increase your income. You can ask for a raise or maybe look for a higher paying job. Either of the two are decent suggestions. I would advise against working overtime or finding a second job. The more you work the less time you have to enjoy life. It may help you to keep the lifestyle you have, but it's affecting your work/life balance. If you have to work overtime or take a second job temporarily in order to pay off a debt than that's not a bad option. You don't want to be permanently stuck working additional hours in order to maintain high expenses. If you can find a way to generate more income while reducing your expenses than you've found a winning combination.

Let's get back to cash flow. Once you've written down and subtracted expenses from your income you are left with your discretionary income. Now you must decide how you want to divide it up. As I stated earlier, be sure to 'pay yourself first'. Transfer a portion of your discretionary income to a savings account. Allow yourself a portion to cover miscellaneous expenses such as entertainment. The next portion of your budget is where you decide how to become debt free. I suggest you use a large amount of your discretionary income to pay down debt. I used this method but only after setting money aside in an emergency fund.

As discussed previously the best way to reduce debt is to pay larger amounts of principal. Make a list of your debts as well as their interest rates. You should work at paying off one debt at a time while making minimum payments on your other debts. It's best to start with the loan with highest interest rate which is usually credit card debt. My exception to this rule is if you have a situation where you have a higher interest rate loan with a high balance and another loan with a small balance. For example, let's say you have a credit card balance of $25,000 and a car loan with a remaining balance of $7,000. Even though the credit card has a higher interest rate it may make sense to pay principal toward the car loan first. You'll pay off the car loan sooner and free up cash that you can then devote to paying down the credit card. Once you've paid down the credit card you can move on to the next debt.

My road to becoming debt free began with a mortgage. I was fortunate enough to make it through college with no credit card, car loan or student loan debt. I started working out of college and within a year financed a condo. I took out a 30 year bi-weekly mortgage and paid additional principal when making payments. This was my only debt for a couple of years until I got married. My wife and I discussed finances and were aware of one another's debts before getting married. I very strongly suggest you discuss finances and especially existing debt with a potential spouse. It would be an unpleasant surprise to marry someone and find out afterwards they had large financial obligations since you essentially inherit your spouse's debt. At that time my wife and I had a small car loan, moderate student loan debt and a mortgage. The dollar amounts were vastly different but I believe the interest rate on the student loan debt was higher than the car loan. However, the car loan was easily the smallest (just under $10,000) so we budgeted as much as we comfortably could to pay down the car loan. I still remember how good it felt to make that final payment.

Now that we had freed up some cash we began using that extra money to pay down student loans. It took time but we stuck with our budget and sure enough paid off the student loans. We then directed that money towards making larger mortgage payments since this was our only other debt. About eighteen months before paying off the condo I used a home equity line of credit to refinance the mortgage. There were no closing costs, the interest rate was much lower and the first mortgage was being paid off. It took about seven years from getting married to paying off our condo but we did it. I loved being debt free but it was short lived as my wife and I had a growing 4 year old at the time and the condo was pretty small.

      We shopped for about two years and eventually found a nice but moderate sized house that was just what we needed. My wife and I decided to rent out our condo for a while which added to the income side of our budget. I really wanted to take out a 15 or 20 year mortgage on the house but it was a new debt, and our largest ever, and we wanted to make sure we were comfortable and not stretching our budget too much. So we took out another 30 year bi-weekly mortgage. This was our only loan so we budgeted as much additional principal as we could. A year later we were settled and comfortable with our new budget. I found a low cost mortgage refinance program and refinanced to a 15 year term. Unfortunately, the program would not allow bi-weekly payments, so I decided to just make additional principal payments every couple weeks. Since graduating college we both worked and advanced in our careers and our income grew. We continuously increased our additional principal payments to the mortgage until we finally paid it off. This was an even greater feeling of accomplishment because the house offers enough space for us to live our entire life if we choose. The condo was a bit different because we knew it was not permanent. The freedom of having our house paid off was worth every bit of sacrifice and it was only made possible by creating and sticking to a budget.

IX. Determination, Commitment, Self-Control

Now that you've created a budget you have to make it work. It's important the budget you created is realistic in order for you to achieve the short and long term goals you've set. As I stated previously, sticking to a budget requires a significant amount of sacrifice. You have to be motivated and determined to make every effort possible to accomplish what you've set out to achieve. That may mean a tighter entertainment or vacation budget than you're used to. It could mean keeping your old not so pretty car longer. You could have a group of friends that want to plan a long weekend getaway and it just may not be in your budget. Whatever it is, you have to keep your long-term vision.

You can set the budget as flexible as you'd like. Maybe your plan to become debt free doesn't have to be a ten year plan. You can make it a twelve or thirteen year plan and that's perfectly okay. These are your goals and your life, so don't make yourself so uncomfortable that you feel like you're not living. I have a pretty high threshold for sacrifice. I think part of it is that I'm a fairly simple person and find happiness in the little things. Some of the most relaxing activities I enjoy are hiking, fishing, walking and taking my son to the park. They are also very inexpensive activities which helps me to keep my entertainment budget down. Once you've established good spending habits you have to continue to exercise self-control and stay committed. It's probably easier today than ever before to spend excessively with internet shopping and app stores on your cell phone. You may find an item online and with a few clicks it's charged to your credit or debit card. Smart phones have made it very easy with all the different types of apps and in app purchases that can be made. Some purchases can even be added to your cell phone bill. This is all by design because the sales and marketing world is trying to get your money. If you're committed to operating within your budget you'll have to exercise a great deal of self-control.

      Staying committed to a budget can be very challenging because big financial goals take years to accomplish. My wife and I have always talked about the things we'd like to do that we haven't been able to afford. Those types of conversations usually led us to look to our debt free future when we would be more financially comfortable. Like I said before, you can't put everything off forever because we only have one chance at this life. For example, my wife and I discussed taking our son to Disneyworld for many years. We wanted to wait until he was a good age to enjoy and remember the trip but also for us to be able to budget for it. We wound up taking our first big family trip to Disney not too long before our budget allowed us to pay off our house. It wasn't the ideal time to spend that money when we were so close to our goal. However, it was perfect timing in our life and it was well worth the investment in our family. We had an awesome time and were thrilled with our financial decision. These are the types of situations I was referring to when I said to leave room in your budget and make sure you enjoy life.

Trying to be cautious with money can also carry its share of judgment from others. This is something you have to learn to accept. I consider myself a frugal person and have received some criticism for it. It is often misconstrued with being cheap and carries a negative connotation. However, being frugal is defined as being economical, not wasteful and prudently saving or sparing. It took me a long time to realize that being frugal is actually a very positive thing. I think it's smart to not be wasteful with anything, whether it's money, food, water or even time. I've never met a frugal person that was struggling financially. If you really want your budget to work you have to be economical and thrifty.

X. Reaping the Reward

After you get used to your budget you figure out how to comfortably operate within its guidelines. The toughest part about staying committed is that it's not always easy to stay focused on the end goal which can be fairly long term. It's always useful to have short and long term goals. It keeps us driven and rewards us with a feeling of achievement. Once my wife and I reached our goal of becoming debt free we had to alter our budget. We had devoted such a large portion of income to paying off debt and once it was gone we had a significant amount of free cash flow. What a great feeling it was to finally be debt free!

When we were creating a new budget we decided there needed to be much more flexibility than our previous budget. It was pretty tight because we decided to make more sacrifice in order to achieve our goal sooner rather than later. It was worth it but it was time to reap the rewards of being debt free. This took me some getting used to and I found I had to train and allow myself to spend money a little more freely. It doesn't mean not to save and to splurge like crazy. It just means realizing you don't have the financial obligations you once had and it's okay to spend money on some of the extras you used to pass on.

Our budget included more retirement, investment and college savings. However, the very best part of the new budget was planning for more vacations and saving toward a newer car. These things are fun to think about and were now very realistic short-term goals. I hope this type of life is intriguing to you because who doesn't want more financial freedom. If you're unhappy with your current financial situation it doesn't have to stay that way. You are in control of your financial future and I know you can do it. Thank you for reading and sharing in my life experiences. I hope my experience as well as the information I've provided will help you to begin or even continue your journey to becoming debt free.